How to Make a Mudpie

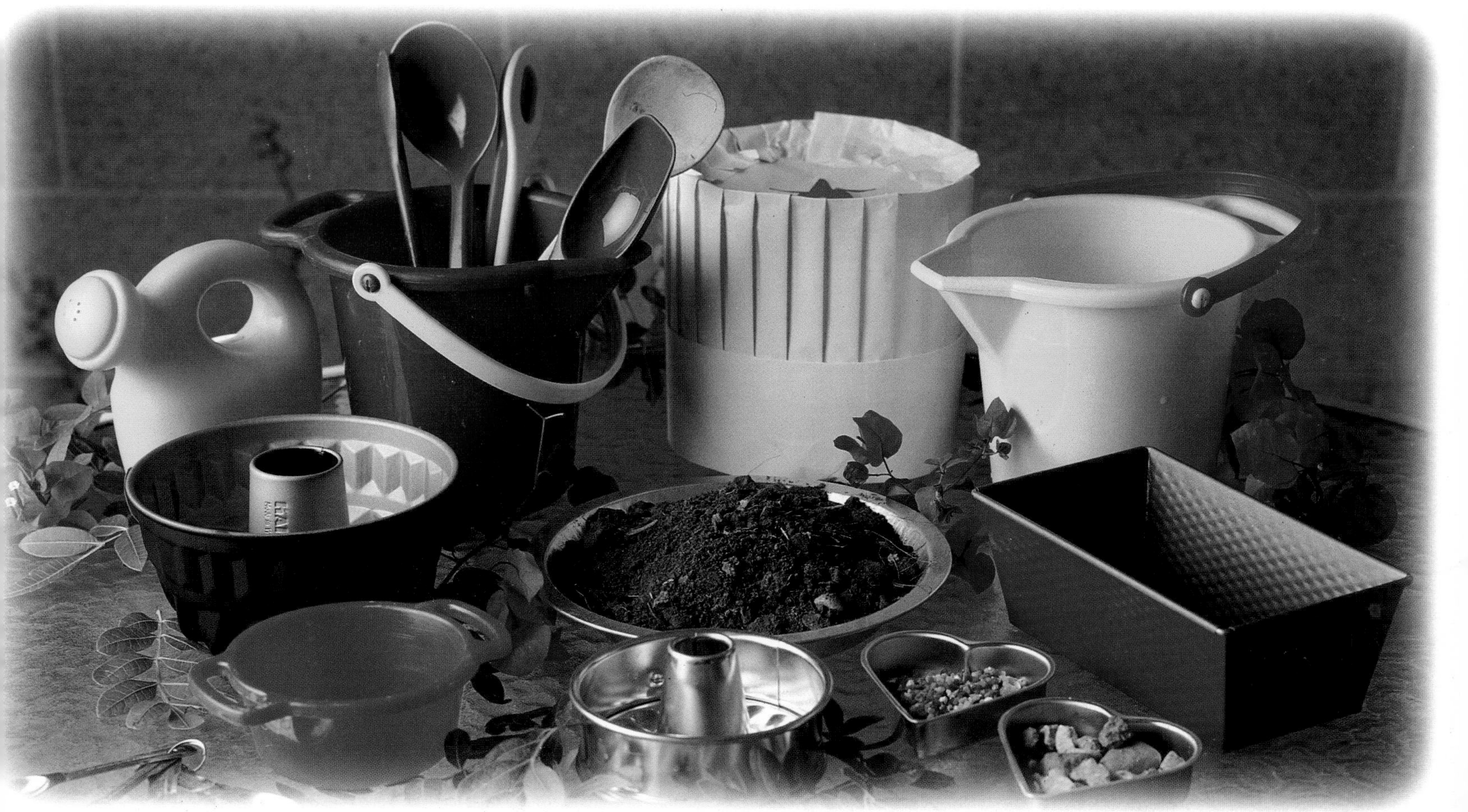

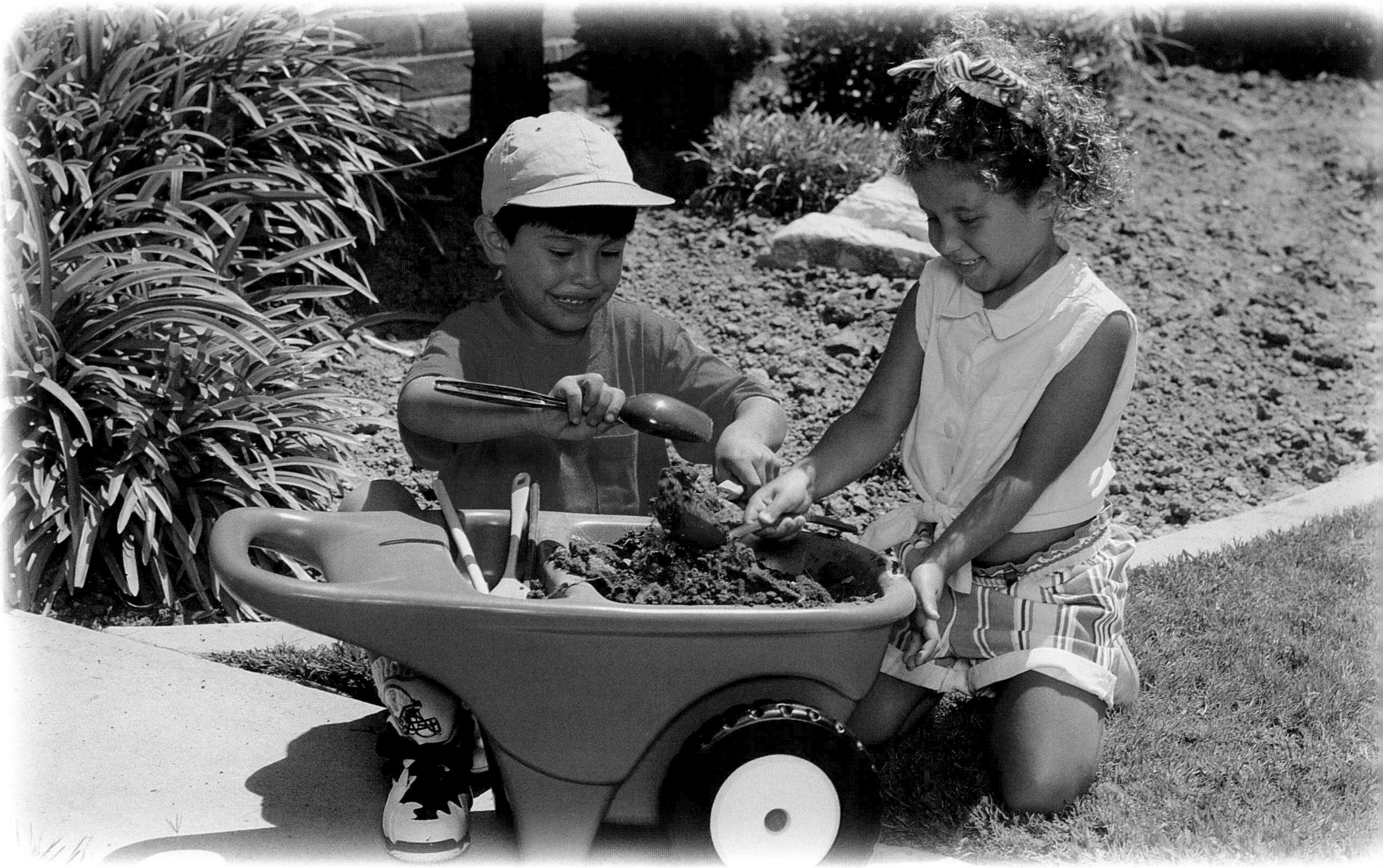

You need some dirt.

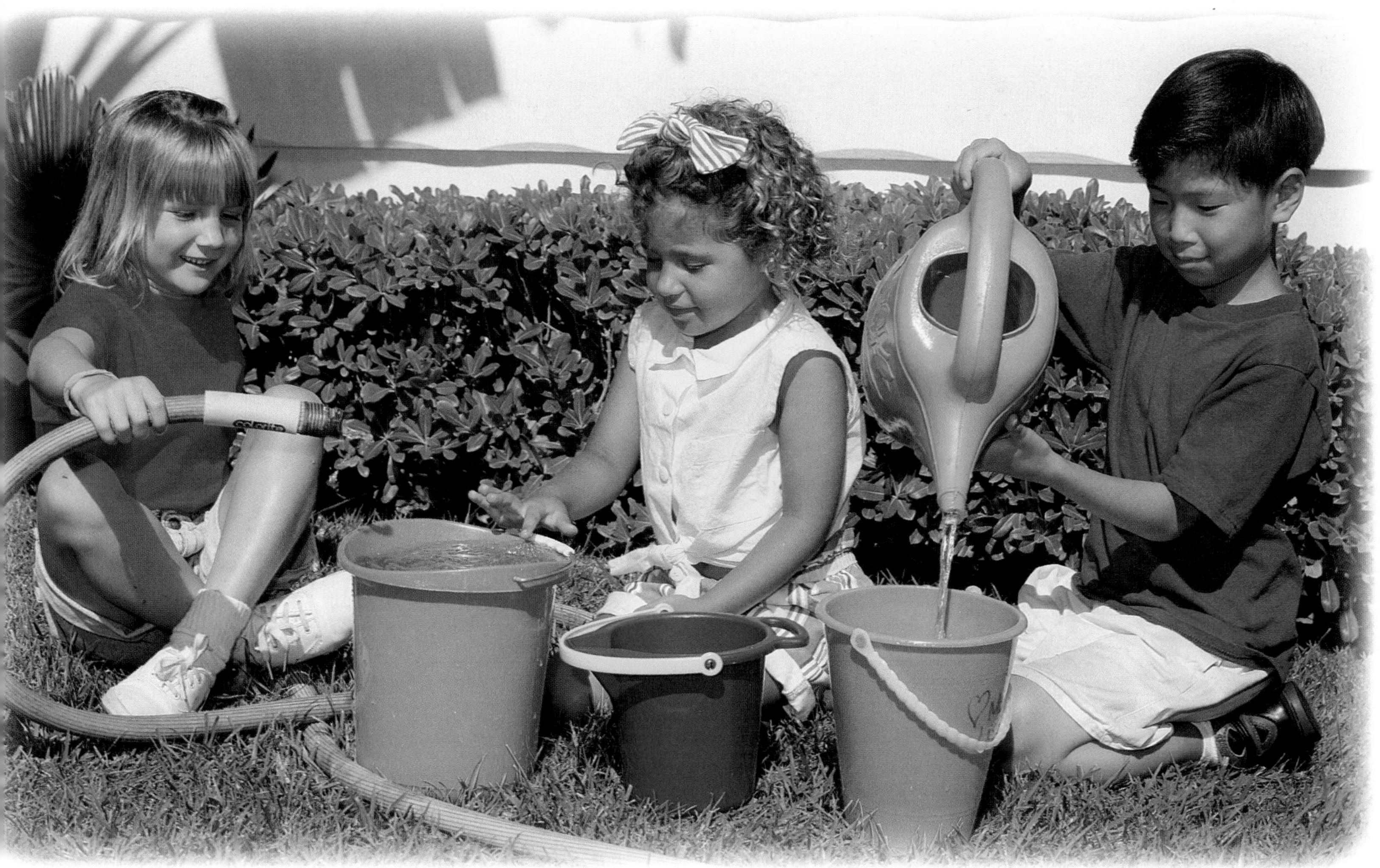

You need some water.

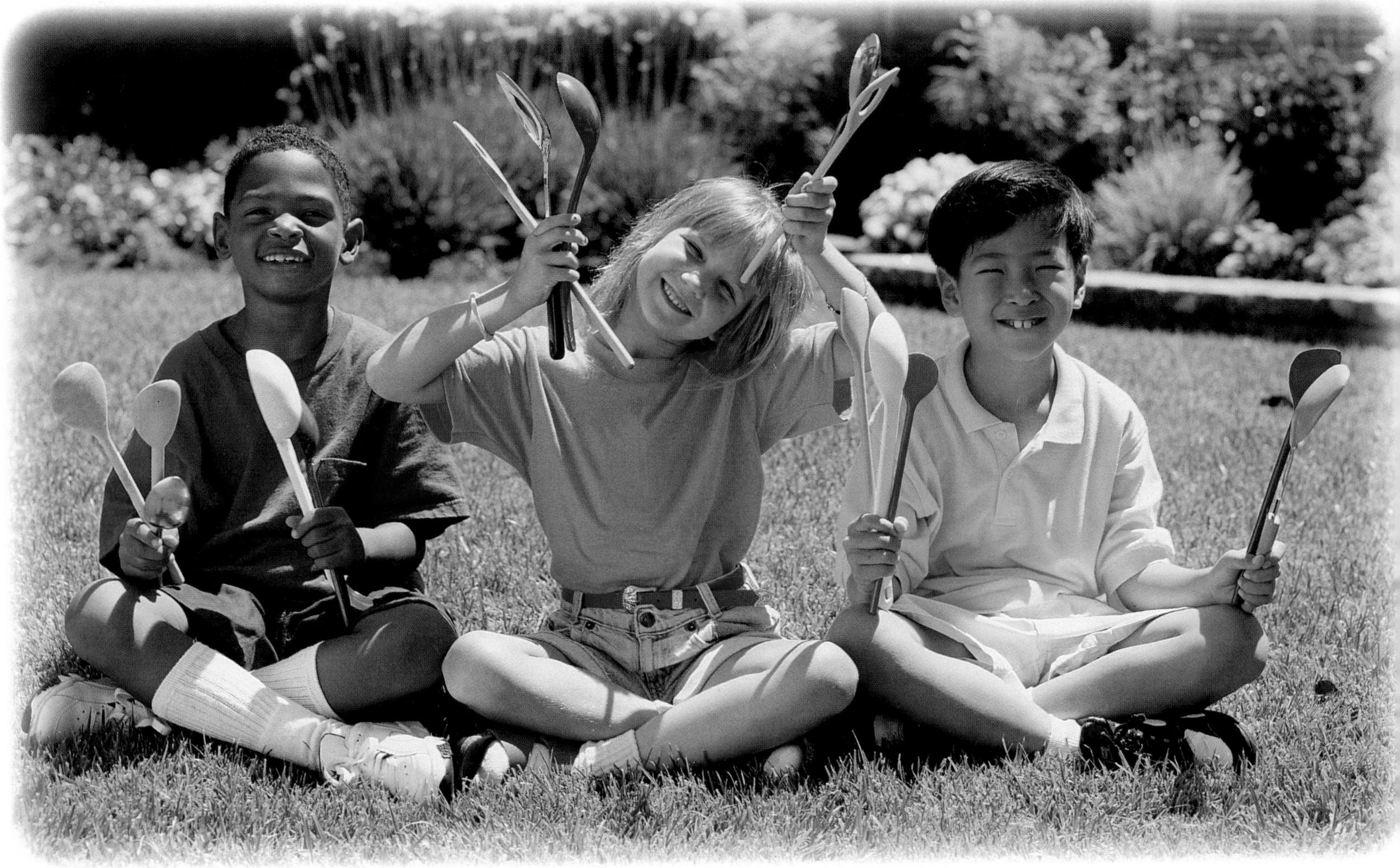

You need some spoons.

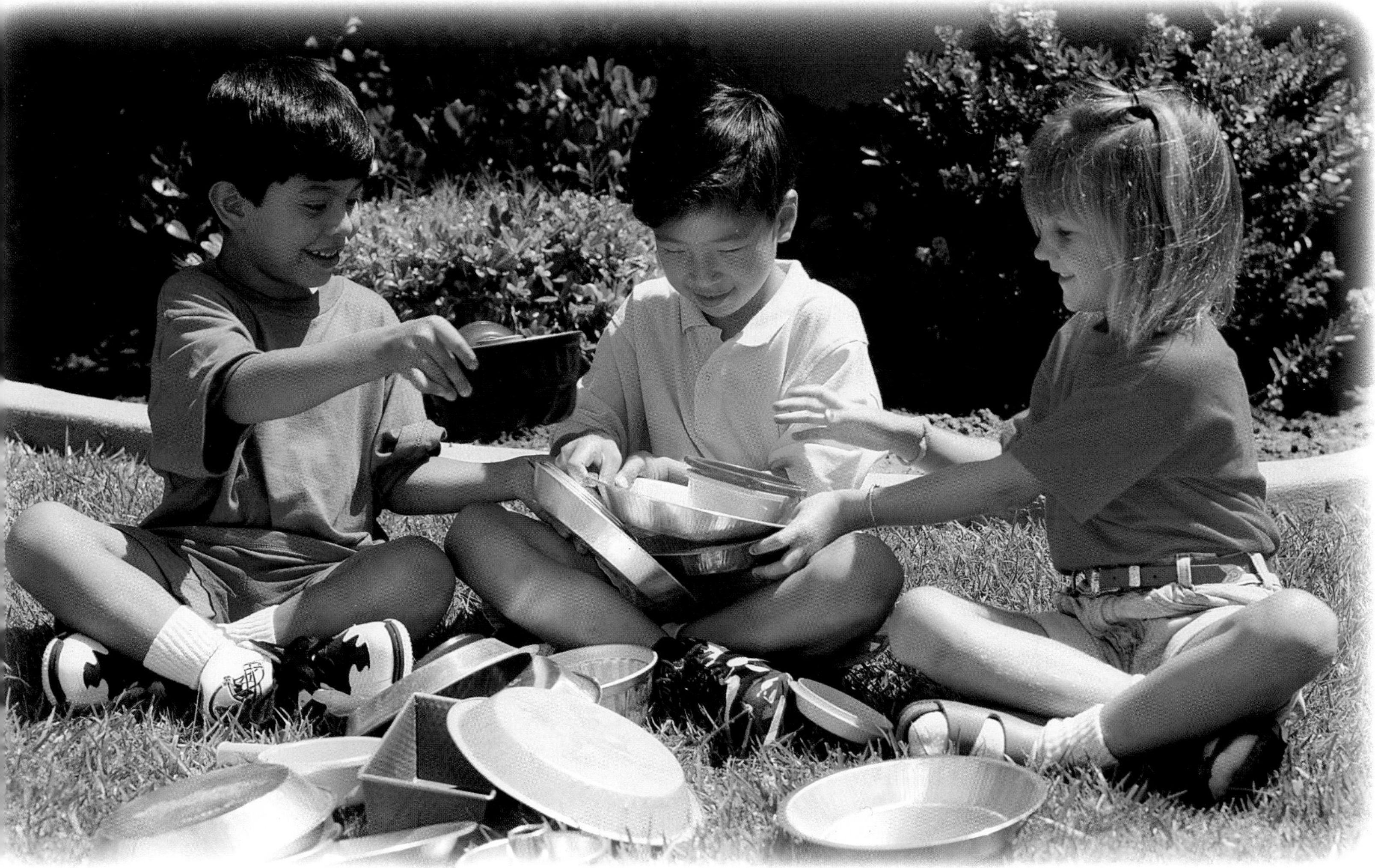

You need some pans.

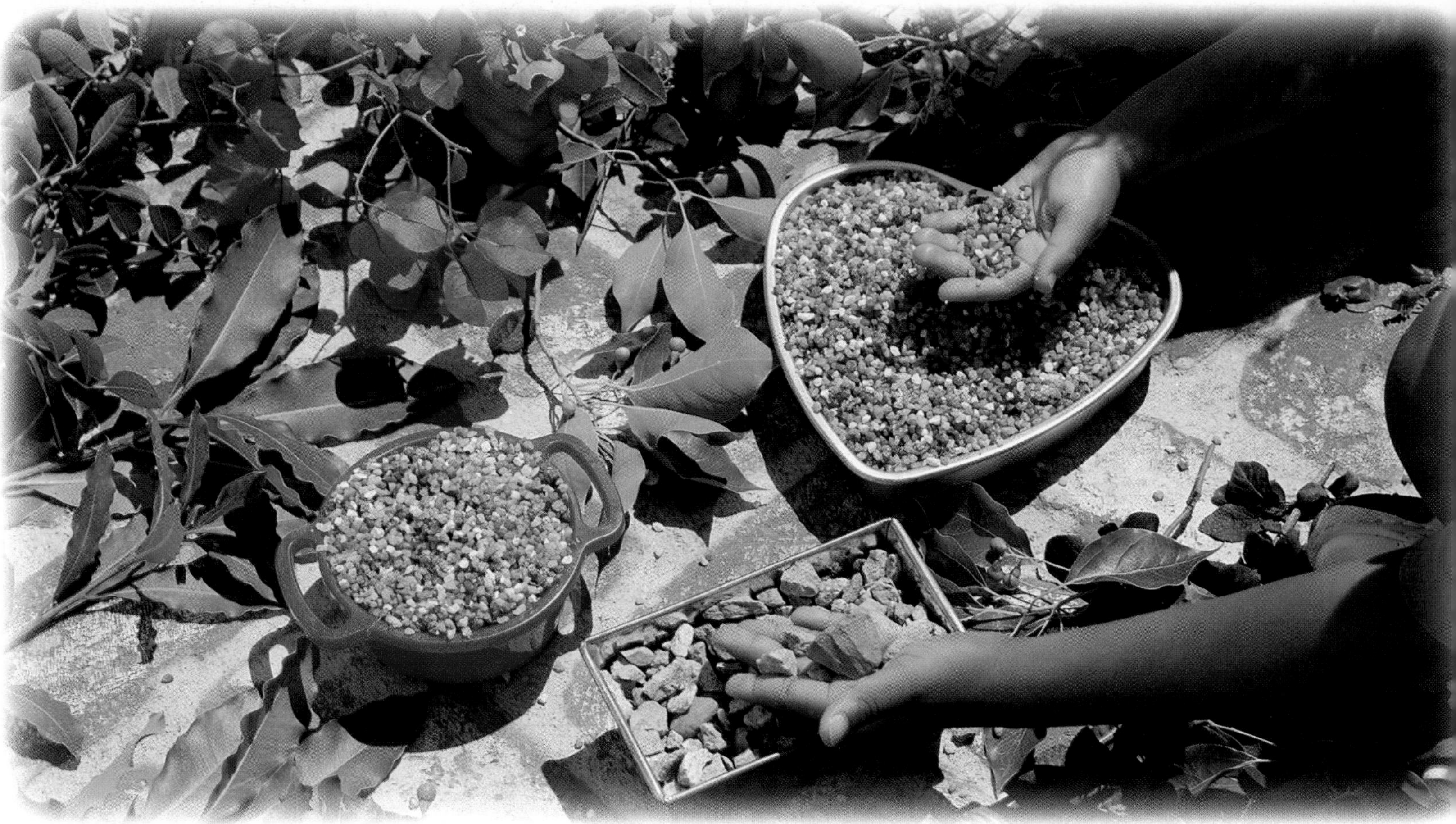

You need some stones.
You need some leaves.

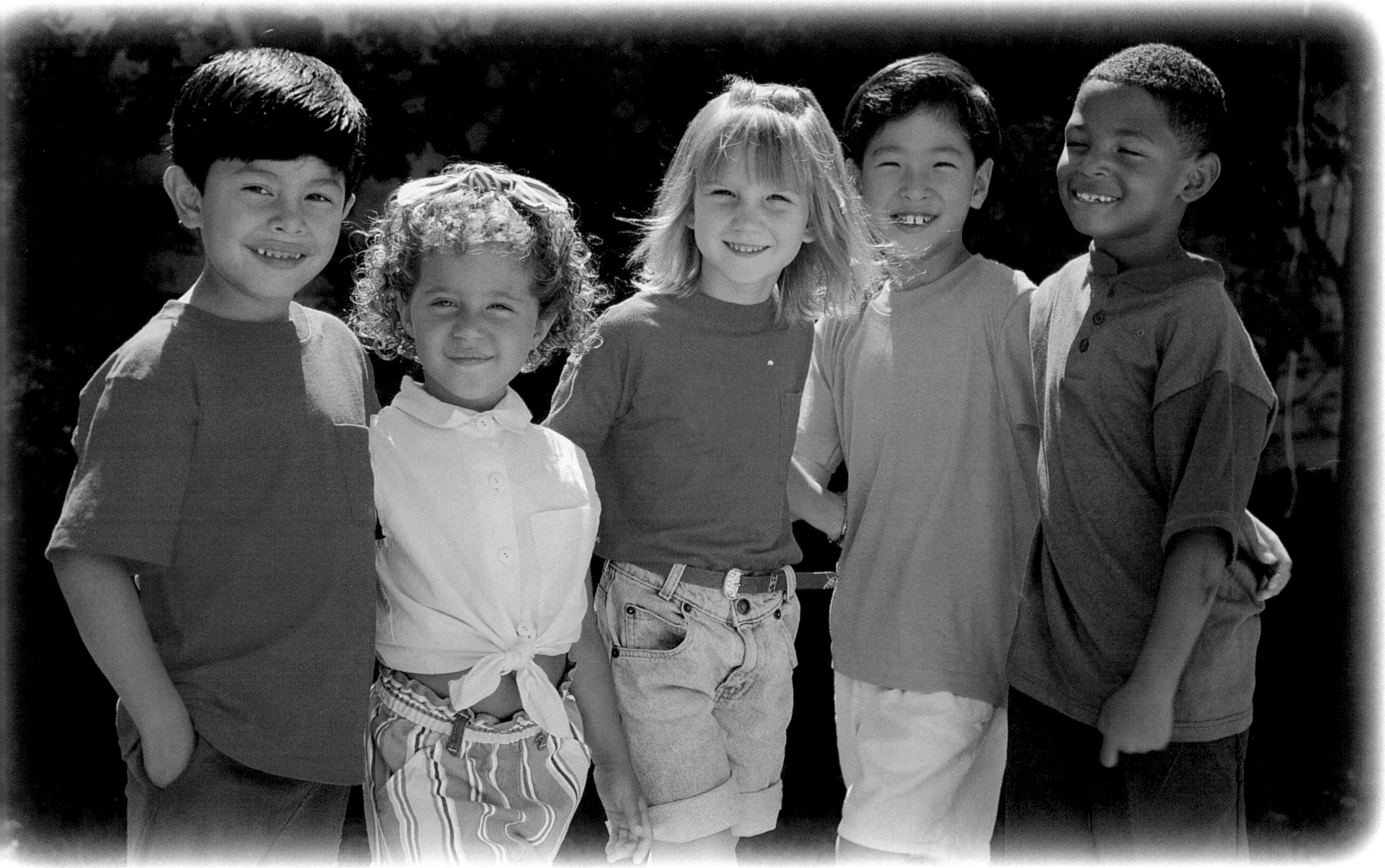

You need some kids.

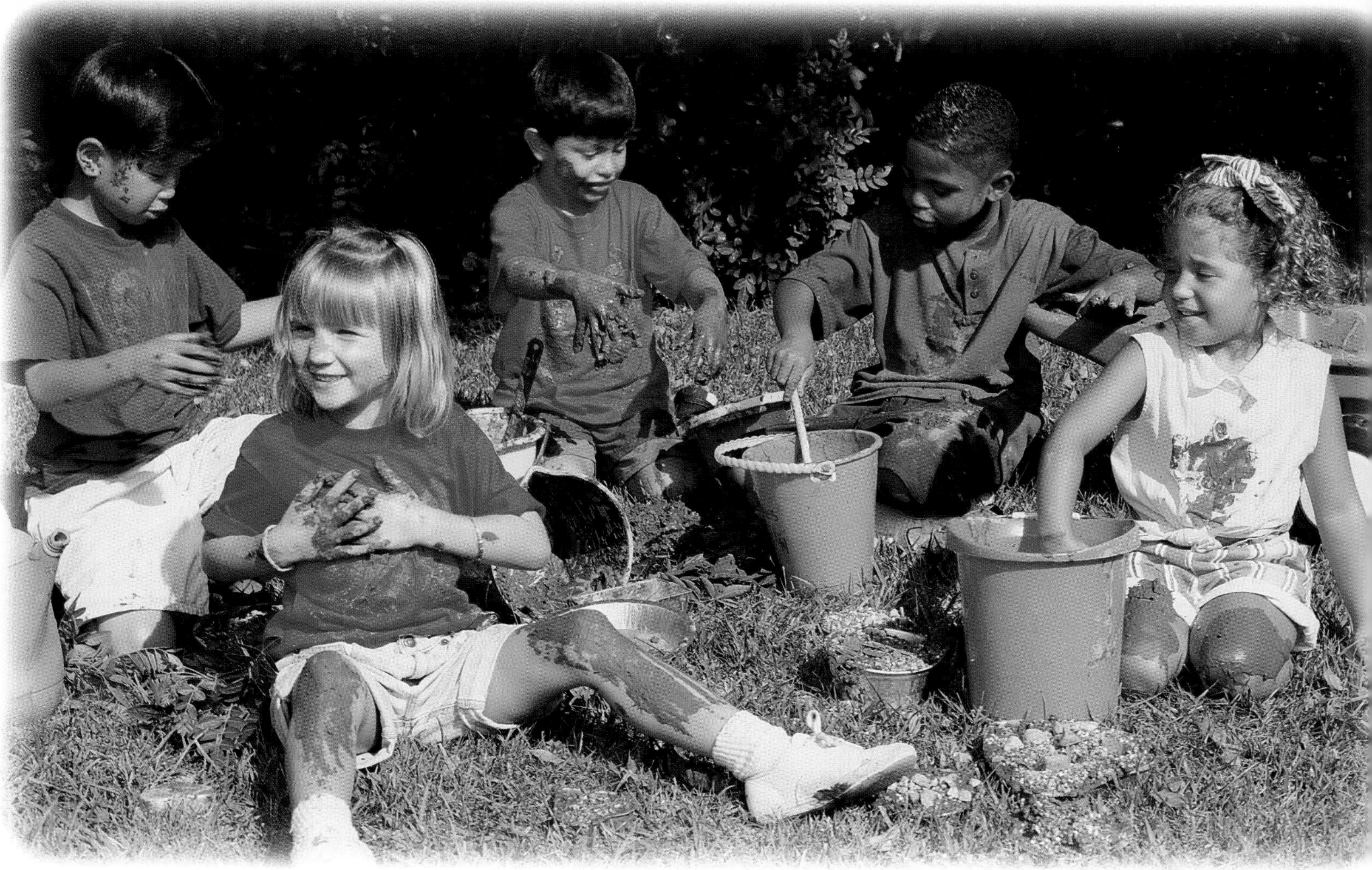

You need some soap!